A Day With
HOMO SAPIENS

LIFE 15,000 YEARS AGO

DR. FIORENZO FACCHINI

A Day With HOMO SAPIENS

LIFE 15,000 YEARS AGO

Illustrations by
GIORGIO BACCHIN

TWENTY-FIRST CENTURY BOOKS / BROOKFIELD, CONNECTICUT

English translation copyright © 2003 by Twenty-First Century Books
Originally published by Editoriale Jaca Book spa
Via Gioberti 7,
20123, Milano, Italy
www.jacabook.it

CIP data is on file at the Library of Congress
0-7613-2768-1 (lib. bdg.)

Published by Twenty-First Century Books
A Division of The Millbrook Press, Inc.
2 Old New Milford Road
Brookfield, Connecticut 06804
www.millbrookpress.com

Printed in Italy
2 4 5 3 1

CONTENTS

Foreword

6

Introduction

Entering the World of *Homo Sapiens Sapiens*

7

Mabuk's Day

19

Glossary

44

Index

47

Picture Credits

48

FOREWORD

This volume is the last in a series that has helped us to imagine the daily life of the most ancient beings of the genus we call *Homo*. In the stage of development called *Homo sapiens sapiens*, humans are similar to those of today. In this series, we have learned about early man's physical changes as well as changes in his behavior, in particular that unique behavior that can be called culture. In this last volume, arrows, which we call arrows of cultural evolution, point from portrayals of the realities in the life of *Homo sapiens sapiens* to pictures from long-gone times and places that show how our ancestors developed. Cultural expression takes humans beyond the fulfillment of physical needs. Culture is what makes houses more than just shelters, but also symbols of the cohesiveness of family; culture is what makes clothing not only protection for the body, but a way in which people express themselves; culture is art, and *Homo sapiens sapiens* was a great artist. In their story, which reaches far back in time, early humans demonstrate the ability to learn things and reflect upon them with conscience. From the beginning, humans have been able to express their culture in a variety of ways, to adapt to their environment without letting it conquer them, and to create new environments and conditions appropriate for social life. Humans are anchored to the biological world, but culture enters into the evolutionary process and can retard or advance human development. Humans create culture, and culture creates the human.

INTRODUCTION

ENTERING THE WORLD
OF *HOMO SAPIENS SAPIENS*

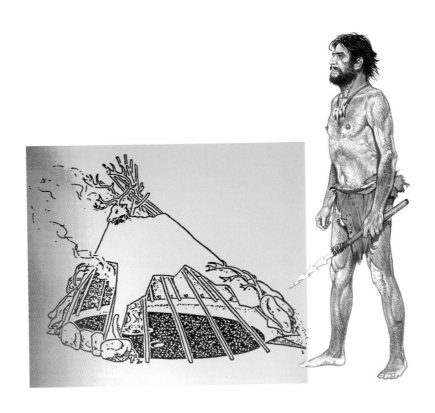

INTRODUCTION

Around 35,000 years ago, the modern-day human being, known as *Homo sapiens sapiens*, lived on all continents. He looked different and behaved differently than earlier humans and had more rich ways of expressing his culture. Facial traits, such as the jutting jaw and supraorbital torus present in *Homo erectus* and

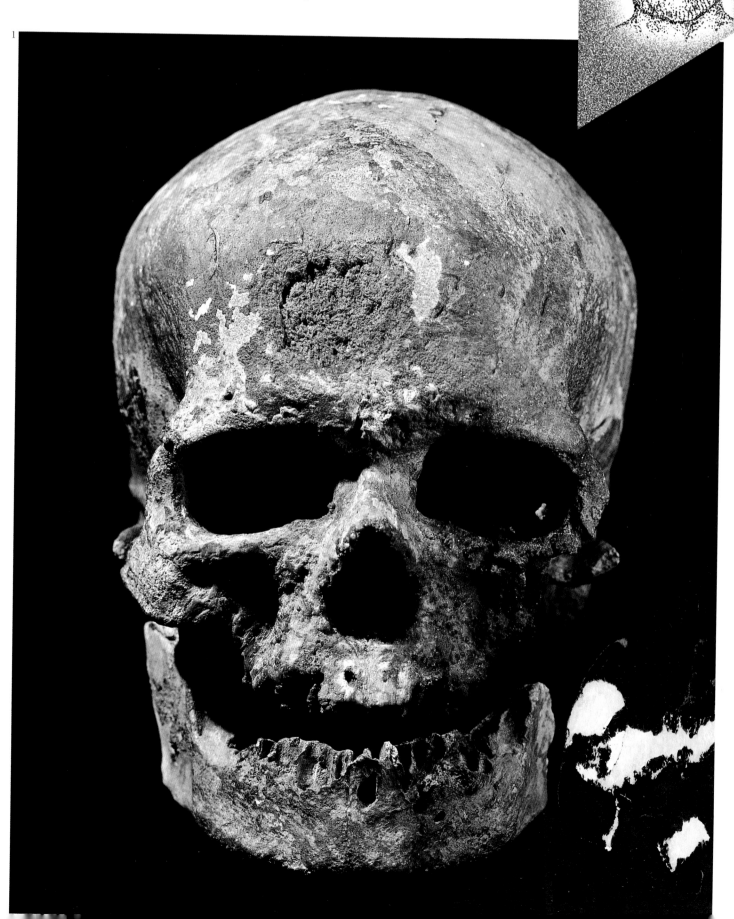

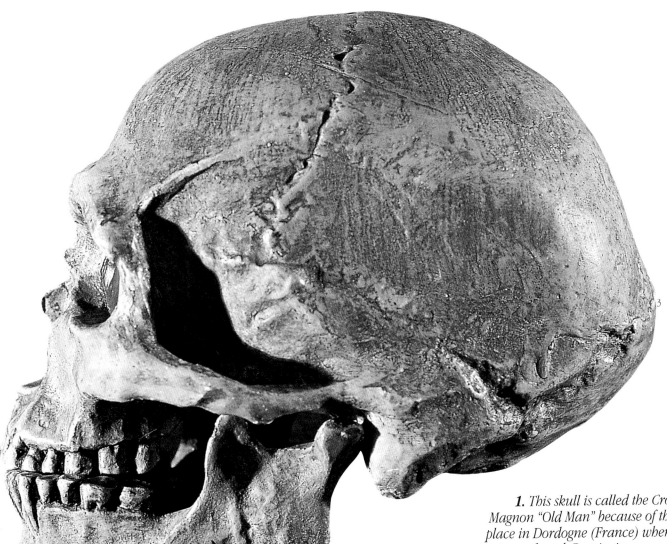

the Neanderthals of Europe and the Near East, disappeared. The head of *Homo sapiens sapiens* was characterized by a high forehead and cranial vault, a gracile facial structure, and a well-developed chin. His lower limbs were also longer. These changes started between 150,000 and 100,000 years ago in Africa. We know this from the remains of *Homo sapiens antiquus* found in Omo (Kenya), Laetoli (Tanzania), and other sites.

Modern humans then moved from Africa to Europe and Asia. In the N~ st, the oldest human remains date from 90,000 years ago an. found in Qafzeh and Skhul (Israel).

~ hi. journey eastward, *Homo sapiens sapiens* went first to the t and Southeast Asia and then moved on to the Americas and str 'a. He reached Europe around 35,000 years ago, moving along the east coast of the Mediterranean and heading north toward Turkey and the Black Sea.

1. This skull is called the Cro-Magnon "Old Man" because of the place in Dordogne (France) where it was found. Despite its name, it was probably the skull of someone not even fifty years old. It is one of the oldest and complete remains of Homo sapiens sapiens *and probably dates from between 30,000 and 28,000 years ago. It has been said that this type of human would have come to Europe from the Middle East or Africa.*

2. Here we see the reconstructed face of the Cro-Magnon "Old Man."

3. A skull of Homo sapiens sapiens *found at Predmostí (Czech Republic), a site where evidence of hearths, graves, and numerous examples of prehistoric stone industry have been found, along with decorated pieces of ivory and bone, small figurines, and other decorative items dating from about 26,000 years ago. The skulls found there were those of* Homo sapiens sapiens, *although, like other remains from the same epoch in central and eastern Europe, they have some characteristics of Neanderthal humans.*

Homo sapiens sapiens probably gradually substituted *Homo erectus* of Asia and the European Neanderthals, but he could also have been a partial mixture of both. In any case, this new human form eventually became the dominant one.

The theory that modern humans originated in Africa is supported by the findings of DNA analysis in modern-day Africans. This research suggests that modern humans stem from one family tree, which originated in Africa, about 200,000–150,000 years ago. This theory, called *substitution theory*, does not agree with *continuity theory*, which suggests that *Homo sapiens* evolved from local *Homo erectus* forms in the different regions.

The climate that *Homo sapiens sapiens* endured in the Northern Hemisphere was rather severe because of the glaciers that covered vast regions.

1. *Spear points found in various sites in North America from about 12,000 to 8,000 years ago. In the late stages of the Paleolithic age, stone industry became more refined with the production of thinner blades and bladelets. The longest among those in this photo measures 3 inches.*

2. *Other tools that show the technological evolution of* Homo sapiens sapiens *are harpoons, which are used for spearing fish. The drawing shows some that are made from reindeer antler. Little by little, they became more specialized, with different types of barbs.*

3. *A point securely mounted on a wooden handle that can be used for hunting or for self-defense.*

4. *The bow: a flexible, curved strip of wood which, with the spring of a tightened cord tied to each end, allows an arrow placed in the middle of the cord to be propelled with a good amount of speed.*

Modern humans of the European Upper Paleolithic showed an increasing ability to work flint. Their high technology allowed them to make small precision tools: a wide range of very thin blades and bladelets, points and burins. As a result, the same amount of raw material could yield a greater number of tools.

Apart from flint, bone and the horns of animals (such as reindeer, deer, and mammoths) were of great use. Men made harpoons for fishing and spear-throwers for propelling javelins. The bow appeared about 15,000 years ago.

Social life developed not only in outdoor settlements but also in sheltered spaces such as caves. Caves were not used for dwelling, but for rituals connected with group life. Cave walls have revealed paintings that depict hunts and animals such as bison,

5. *Javelins could be propelled greater distances and with greater strength using a mechanism made from wood, bone, or horn. The spear thrower had a central body with a hook or thong on the end on which the javelin was positioned. The javelin was released from the mechanism at the moment it was launched. The greater the strength of the thrust, the better the tool was for wounding prey. The spear thrower, which was also called an "atlatl," was a basic tool for hunters in North America, 12,000 to 10,000 years ago.*

6, 7, 8. *Pierced canine teeth, ornamental pendants from about 30,000 years ago found in Kostienki (Russia). In the drawing we see the bear and the fox, whose canines were most commonly used for making these types of pendants.*

horses, and rhinoceroses. These pictures are good indicators of the rich symbolism of rites that probably had propitiatory magic purposes.

Homo sapiens sapiens represented human figures—especially feminine, the so-called Venus—and animal figures, sculpting and engraving them on plaquettes of stone, bone, and antler, or on cave walls. He also depicted figures that are part animal and part human, which may have been shamans.

Funeral practices, already known by the Neanderthals, continued to evolve, and were enriched with more objects (small items like animal parts or shells) being buried with the corpse. This funerary equipment had some symbolic meaning for the next life.

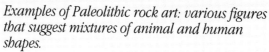

Examples of Paleolithic rock art: various figures that suggest mixtures of animal and human shapes.

1. The mysterious figure called "The Sorcerer," with large antlers and a tail. In its semi-upright position, with human feet, it seems to be staring at something. It was found in the Trois Frères cave in Ariège (France).

2. An engraved figure, from the Altamira Cave (Spain), which appears to be a man with his arms raised, wearing an animal mask.

3, 4. Men, with weapons and tools, wearing bull masks, from Racó de Molero and El Cingle de la Mola Remigia (Spain).

Because of their hunting and gathering lifestyle, humans did not settle long in any single place. The length of time they stayed anywhere depended upon how long the resources there lasted. And with a wider range of finer tools, people were equipped to move around their environment more easily.

The abundant forests were filled with animals adapted to a cold climate, such as bison, mammoths, deer, bears, and beavers. The deer were useful not only for their meat but also for their skins and antlers. The mammoth supplied food as well as ivory tusks that were used for making tools and portable art pieces, such as engraved plaquettes. Evidence of huts made with mammoth bones has been found.

Fire was used for preparing food, which made the food easier to consume. It was also used to illuminate caves.

5

5. *Fitting together stone fragments found in a cave, called Apollo 11, in South Namibia (southern Africa). The painted animal appears to be a feline to which human limbs have been added. It dates from about 30,000 years ago.*

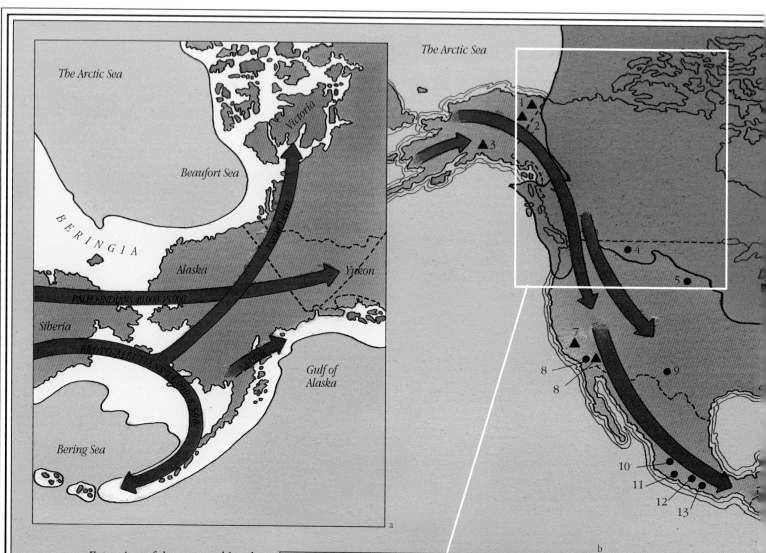

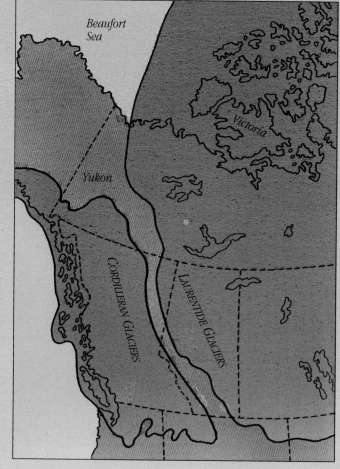

a. Extension of the emerged land (Beringia) that linked Asia and the North American continent and the probable migratory paths leading out of Asia. The Paleo-Indians went toward the Yukon territory at various times during the period between 40,000 and 15,000 years ago. Between 14,000 and 8,500 years ago, there was a migratory stream out of Asia that broke off into different branches: the ancestors of the Eskimo, who went to the Northwest, the Proto-Aleutians, who settled in the Aleutian Archipelago, and the ancestors of the Na-Dene (Northwest Indians).

b. During the last Ice Age, around 15,000 years ago, a strip of land was formed, linking the Yukon, in Canada, to the northern part of the United States between the Cordilleran Glaciers to the West and the Laurentide Glaciers to the East. This strip of land allowed large mammals, such as mammoth and bison, and humans, to pass through and to travel to the southern regions. The white square on the large map shows the location of this small map.

1. Old Crow (27,000)
2. Bluefish (15-12,000)
3. Dry Creek (15-12,000)
4. Taber (40,000)
5. Minnesota (10,000)
6. Meadowcroft (19-14,000)
7. La Jolla (21,500)
8. Santa Rosa (30,000?)
8. Santa Rosa (29,000)
9. Midland (8,600)
10. Astahuacan (9,000?)
11. Chicoloapan (7,000)
12. Tlapacoya (22,000)
13. Tepexpán (11,000)
14. Muaco (14,250)
15. Punin (10,000)
16. Pikimachay (14,000)
17. Lagoa Santa (10,000)
18. Confins (Upper Pleistoc.)
19. Los Toldos (12,600)

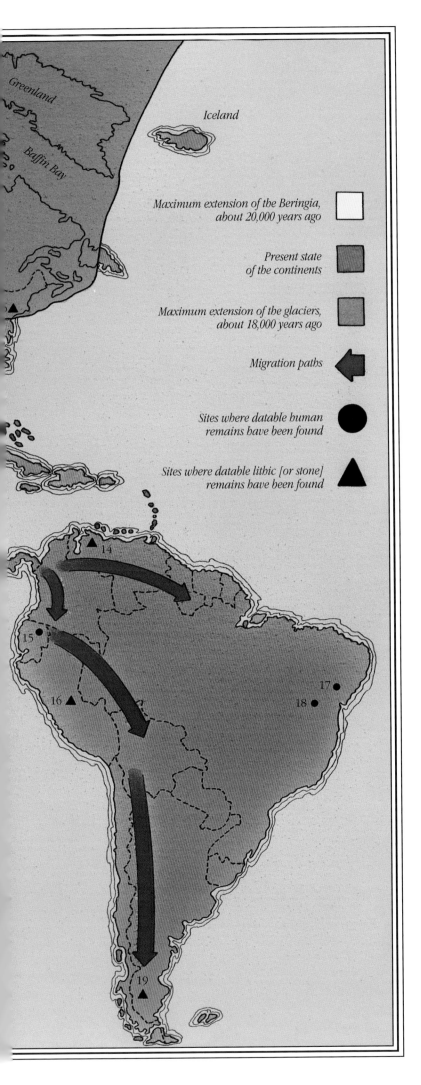

During the *Homo sapiens sapiens* phase, humans moved from Asia to the Americas and Australia. This migration was possible because of the configuration of the continents at that time. During the last Ice Age, the bodies of water that separate Australia and the Americas from Asia were different from the way they are today. The sea level was lower, which allowed a land bridge (called Beringia) to emerge in what is now the Bering Strait. Along this strip of land, groups of humans, presumably with herds of animals, passed from East Asia to Alaska and on to the Yukon of North America in various waves, between 40,000 and 10,000 years ago. From there, they moved northeast and to the central and southern regions of the Americas, passing through a corridor of land between the Cordilleran and Laurentide glaciers. The age of the archaeological remains decreases from north to south. Other small contributions were made to the

1. *Probable extension of the glaciers in North America during the last Ice Age, about 70,000 to 10,000 years ago. The sea level dropped and a "bridge" of land (Beringia) emerged between Asia and the North American continent. Around 18,000 years ago, the glaciers reached their maximum expansion up to the present-day borders of Canada and the United States. There were also alternating phases of glacial regression and expansion that may have played a role in the movement of humans and animals.*

Legend (from map):

Maximum extension of the Beringia, about 20,000 years ago

Present state of the continents

Maximum extension of the glaciers, about 18,000 years ago

Migration paths

Sites where datable human remains have been found

Sites where datable lithic [or stone] remains have been found

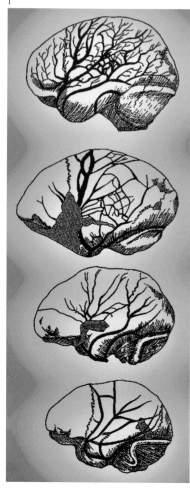

Homo sapiens
sapiens

Neanderthal
Humans

Homo
erectus

Homo
habilis

3. *A skull of* Homo sapiens sapiens *that was found in Java. It dates from the end of the Pleistocene period (15,000–10,000 years ago).*

4. *From Kow Swamp, north of Victoria (Australia): a facial skeleton of* Homo sapiens sapiens *that dates from sometime between 15,000 and 9,000 years ago.*

5. *A skull of* Homo sapiens sapiens *found in Tepexpán (Mexico) with the remaining parts of the skeleton. It appears to be that of a 55-65-year-old man and dates from about 11,000 years ago.*

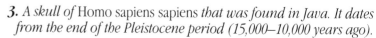

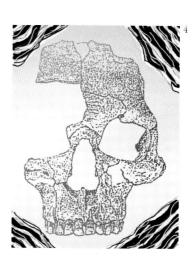

1. 2. *Here we see the evolution of the human brain in a time span just a bit wider than two million years, from* Homo habilis *to* Homo sapiens sapiens. *We can observe that the brain increased not only in size ("cranial capacity") but also in complexity. This observation was made possible because the brain leaves its marks upon bones. So the scientists can take casts of the interior of the skull ("endocranial casts") that reproduce the form of the brain, its convolutions, and its meningeal artery quite clearly. The drawing on the right shows a reconstruction of* Homo sapiens sapiens.

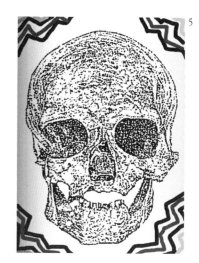

human occupation of the Americas, dating from the post Ice Age period, presumably originating in Southeast Asia and Oceania, and arriving via the Pacific.

With the end of the Ice Age around 10,000 years ago, the sea level changed again and the isthmus of land in the Bering Strait was submerged.

Humans probably arrived in Australia (which, at that time, was connected to New Guinea) from Indonesia about 35,000 years ago. At the time, the body of water that separated Australia from Indonesia must have been much smaller and more shallow, or perhaps there was even a strip of land between Java and the Australian continent.

6. *A wall painting, showing the figure of a bison, from the Paleolithic Altamira Cave (Spain). Because the art found in it is so beautiful, the cave has earned the name "The Sistine Chapel of Prehistory."*

7, 8. *Next to the impressive pictures created by Paleolithic artists, we see the drawings that portray* Homo habilis *and modern man side by side. They look quite different but are also similar in that both are capable of cultural expression.*

MABUK'S DAY

THE MAMMOTH HUNT

Mabuk and his 15-year-old son, Mabuko, are hiding behind a boulder. Early this morning they came with the other men out to the plain, a few miles from the encampment, to hunt a mammoth.

Last night they prepared a trap. They dug a large hole in the ground. Now they are waiting for a herd of mammoths to pass by, going north, as they have always done. The hot season is coming, and the mammoths prefer the cold. As they pass by, they will be driven into the trap and killed.

About fifteen hunters are hiding behind the boulders and in tall grass. They are armed with spears, sticks, and stones. There are also some boys, like Mabuko, who are here to learn how to hunt large animals.

All of a sudden, the men see a large cloud of dust in the distance, and the mammoths appear. They are just like large elephants and have curved tusks and dark, woolly coats.

There are about ten of them. At just the right moment, the men spring out of the hiding places, shout loudly, and swing their sticks about in order to drive the mammoths into the trap. Some of the mammoths fall in, and as they struggle to get out the men attack them. They manage to kill one of the mammoths, which has gotten tangled in the branches in the deep hole.

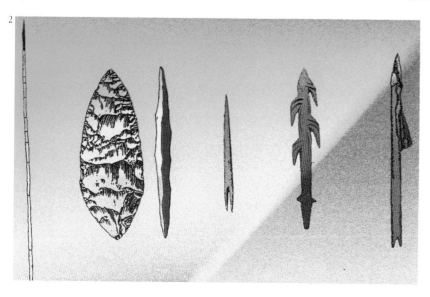

1. The point designed to strike the prey is mounted on a wooden shaft, which is held by the hunter. A groove can be made on the point for inserting it into the shaft; or, vice versa, the groove can be made on the shaft for receiving the point. The two pieces can be fastened together with cord.

2. The drawing shows some examples of the development of hunting weapons. From left: A large wooden javelin with a sharpened tip; a flint point (full face and profile); a bone point with groove; a decorated harpoon with two rows of barbs; and an arrow with a flint point.

3. *A design inspired by the discovery of an entire set of mammoth tusks found near the Manzanares River, not far from Madrid (Spain). Nearby, a drawing of the human figure, drawn to scale, gives us an idea of the colossal size of this Mastodon.*

3

THE MAMMOTH, A GREAT RESOURCE

The hunters are busy butchering the mammoth that they have killed. They are going to bring it back to the encampment. Mabuk tells his son, "The mammoth is our most precious animal, not only for its meat, but also for its bones, tusks, and fur."

"And our huts are made with mammoth parts," Mabuko adds. "We use the skin and the tusks to cover the floor and the hut itself."

Mabuk, his son, and other men volunteer to carry the mammoth's head and the tusks back to the encampment. The other parts of the mammoth will be tied onto strong branches to be carried.

Now the men have finished butchering and are walking home.

During the journey, they notice a herd of reindeer in the distance. "Those animals are also precious," Mabuk explains. "Apart from their meat, they provide us with antlers, which are made of a substance that can be engraved more easily than stone can. We can use it to make hunting tools such as spear-throwers, and also decorative objects for our huts."

1. *Reconstruction of a hut in Mal'ta, Irkutsk (Siberia), decorated with a deer's head. In this site, which dates from about 23,000 years ago, figurines of animals, statuettes of women, and burials with rich ivory funerary equipment were found.*

2. *From Mezhirich (Ukraine), a reconstruction of a mammoth skull painted in red ochre. The site dates from 17,800 and 14,300 years ago and is famous for the many elaborate dwellings where the remains of about 150 mammoths were found. The mammoth was also an artistic resource: interesting mammoth bones and skulls were found painted with geometric designs.*

1

2

3. Ivory blade with an engraved design called "fish scaling" from the site of Timonovka (Russia) dating from between 15,200 and 12,200 years ago. It is thought that these are archival pictographs rather than just decorative objects because ivory fragments were engraved even if they were broken or spoiled.

4. Accumulations of mammoth bone in Milovice (Southern Moravia) in a space reserved for waste, beneath the living area of a group of specialized mammoth hunters dating from between 23,000 to 22,000 years ago.

1. From the Pekarna cave (12,400–11,000 years old) in Moravia, various harpoons made of bone or deer antler. The first has one row of barbs.

2. Two rows of barbs.

3. Three rows of barbs.

4. A sculpture made of reindeer antler 13,000 to 12,000 years ago and showing a fish found in Meiendorf (Germany). The arrow points to examples of how the fish has been used as a symbol of life in various other times and places.

5. A stone, from Lepenski Vir (former Yugoslavia) from around 6000–5500 B.C.E.: the fish-goddess is painted in red, the color of life.

6. A Christian tombstone with the inscription of Licinia, from about 200 C.E. It has an anchor and two fish underneath the Greek inscription "The Fish of Life." The letters that make up the word for "fish" are the first letter of each word in the Greek sentence, "Jesus Christ, Son of God, Savior."

7. Painted fabric of the Senufo tribe (Ivory Coast, Africa): a masked man puts his hands on a large fish. As a symbol of water, which staves off dreaded drought, the fish is one of the sacred animals of the Senufo tribe.

FISHING

The mammoth hunters are on their way back to the encampment.

Mabuk, Mabuko, and other men are carrying their trophy, the mammoth's head. On the way home, they walk by a river.

"Perhaps we'll meet one of our group," says Mabuk. There is a place where the land flattens out and the river widens to form a kind of little lake. At certain times of the year, it is full of fish and boys often go fishing there.

When they arrive at that place, they find some boys trying to catch fish. They corner the fish and then plunge harpoons into their bodies. The harpoon is attached to a rope, and once it penetrates the fish's body, it can't come out. A tug on the rope gets the fish out of the water.

"Grilled fish is delicious," says Mabuk.

THE ENCAMPMENT

By now, the hunters are near the encampment, which is set up near of cave. In bad weather, the cave provides shelter.

There are seven huts, each one for a family with about three or four children.

The huts are circular and roomy. The floor is made of big, flat mammoth bones. Other large animal bones, held together with poles, form a circular frame that is covered with animal skins. The inside of the hut is nicely laid out with special areas for working and resting.

Food is prepared outside the hut. Two large stones near the entrance of the hut serve as a hearth.

When the hunters come back, there will be a great feast.

1. Supposed bases of round huts from the Middle Paleolithic age on the Har Kakom plateau, on the Sinai Peninsula.

2. A different type of ancient hut dating from 25,000 years ago, in Dolní Vestonice (Czech Republic). Here we see a hunter using an indoor hearth to harden clay into a statuette.

3. Reconstruction of a mammoth bone hut (around 15,000 years old) at Mezin (Ukraine). The arrows point to examples of the role of the dance and feast in different times and places.

4. A familiar scene in rock art of Northeast Brazil (9,000 years old) depicting a dance step.

5. A dance scene shown in rock art in central Arabia from the third millennium B.C.E. Dance is a way of celebrating a happy occasion.

6. A man and three women are dancing. Sounds and rhythms are symbolized by the dots over their heads. Dancing was a part of the feast. It reinforced the feeling of togetherness and served to restore everyone physically and emotionally (rock engraving from about 850–700 B.C.E., Val Camonica, Italy).

7. Indian dancers, probably Apache (rock art from the eighteenth century), appear to be wearing ritual headdresses. Dancing provided relief from the danger of the hunt and exploration.

1. *The present-day entrance to the cave of Niaux, Ariège (France), dating from about 12,000 years ago. It is more than 2 kilometers deep inside the mountain, and it is famous for the wonderful paintings—mostly bison and horse—characteristically arranged in panels on its walls. There are also red and black dots and geometric motifs that seem to mark special zones in the complicated topography of the cave, made of halls, chambers, galleries, passageways, recesses, and niches. Evidence attests that the cave had a long period of usage by early modern humans for social purposes.*

2. *A decorated needle from about 20,000 years ago, discovered, along with other pieces of evidence of human life, in the Oblazowa Cave in Poland. The cave may have been a hunting bivouac.*

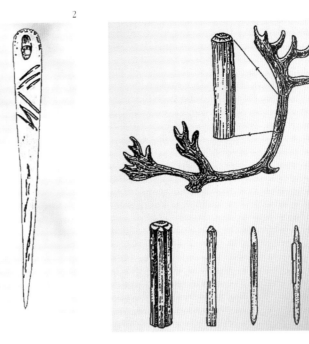

ACTIVITIES IN THE ENCAMPMENT

A portion of the mammoth is given to each family.

Now the women have the job of scraping the hide of the mammoth and preparing the meat for tonight. "We will go to the bison cave to complete the work that we started a few days ago," says Mabuk.

The cave is not far from the encampment. It is called the "bison cave" because the walls have paintings of bison. Bison, like mammoths and reindeer, supply the group with food.

Mabuk's wife, Mabuka, turns to her husband and says, "Before you leave, rest a little and eat these berries that I gathered this morning. I found them growing in the woods."

And so Mabuk sits with his family in front of the hut for a little snack.

3. The drawing shows how typical tools of the end of the Upper Paleolithic, small and thin, were made. A vertical piece of antler is cut off; two parallel engravings are carved in it, in order to detach a segment with a triangular section; this segment is then worked in a pointed-rounded shape and a groove is cut on it; finally, a very small and thin stone blade (called "microblade" or "bladelet") is fitted into the groove. A projectile point has been obtained, sharp as a razor.

4. The black currant, a sweet fruit that is rich in vitamins.

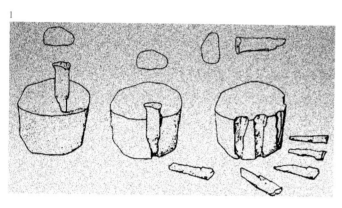

1. Small and thin blades ("microblades" or "bladelets") could also be flaked from flint cores. In the drawing we see how, with the help of an awl and a hammer, small, fine tools used for precision work can be obtained.

2. The drawing depicts a statuette called Venus with the Hood (because its head is covered with a kind of net) from Brassempouy, Lande (France). This bone sculpture dates from about 30,000 to 27,000 years ago.

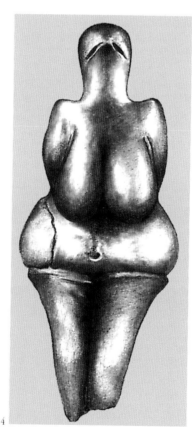

3. This bas-relief from Laussel, the Dordogne (France) dates from a period between 27,000 and 20,000 years ago. It represents an older woman who holds a horn engraved with a series of notches, whose meaning is not known.

4. From Dolní Vestonice (Czech Republic): a statuette in fired clay. It is a woman whose head and limbs are merely sketched but whose body parts related to maternity stand out. It dates from about 25,000 years ago and falls into the category of sculptures of females from that period that were called "Venus." It has been said that they may represent fertility or maternity cults.

A WORKSHOP

Mabuko's brothers, Mabuki and Mabuku, have joined Mabuk and Mabuko. They are eight and twelve years old. When they are older, they will be brought back to the cave again to learn the secrets of the group.

In a bag made from animal skin, they carry a stone lamp and two torches that will light their way in the cave.

On the way, they pass by the group's workshop. It is set up near a rocky outcropping that furnishes the raw material for the group's work. Some men are busy making tools out of flint cores. They have a special method for toolmaking: they use a soft hammer made from a deer's antler to detach from the core very thin blade-shaped flakes.

Mabuk lets his sons watch the others, who are busy working with deer antlers. "Antlers," he says, "are softer than stone and are easier to work with. We can make tools from them for hunting and fishing. We can also engrave on them pictures of the animals we want to hunt. That's one way to have a successful hunt. And antlers can be used for making ornaments such as statuettes of women, to show our respect for motherhood."

1. A Paleolithic artist's lamp. Light is a symbol of knowledge and creativity. It makes those things that are in shadow clear. Let's follow the arrow. 2. The top of a candelabrum from a grave dating from between the seventh and fifth centuries B.C.E., from Chiucchiari, Potenza (Italy). Like other objects found in ancient tombs, this piece shows the living person's desire to accompany the dead person, not in the darkness (death) but in light (life). 3. A picture of a Vietnamese lamp (about 250–110 B.C.E.) in a tomb at Dong Son. 4. A lamp from the third century C.E. in the shape of a basilica. Light celebrates a new "vision" of life.

INTO THE CAVE

We are at the entrance to the cave. Now the lamp and torches are taken from the bag.

The torches are made with resin. The lamp is made of soft stone; it has a shallow hole filled with animal fat.

The opening to the cave is easy to enter, but then it gets narrower. "Duck down a bit," says Mabuk, "because the passageway is very tight."

Crouching, Mabuk and his three sons move ahead carefully, one behind the other. At a certain point, the passageway widens. Mabuk stops; he takes out two stones he has been carrying and rubs them together, making a few sparks. He lights the torches that the boys are holding. "We will light the lamp when we are further along," he says.

The light from the torches reveals a fairly large space, but this is not the end of the journey. Still deeper, there is a narrow opening, which Mabuk and the boys can only enter one at a time.

"Now we are about to enter the great room of the cave," warns Mabuk. "Pay attention to what is off to your right. Before you enter, you will see red and black marks on the wall. They are a sign that we are going into the most important part of the cave."

5. Red and black signs in a passageway of the Altamira Cave (Spain). In many Upper Paleolithic caves, numerous "abstract" signs (dots, lines, clubs, and a variety of more elaborate forms) have been found, sometimes scattered about amongst the "realistic" animal figures, sometimes separated from them. Scientists made different hypotheses to explain their meaning.

THE CAVE ARTISTS

After going through a narrow passage, Mabuk and his sons enter a large space lit by lamps. There they find two of the men from their group busily painting on the cave walls. They have made wooden scaffolding so that they can easily climb up and paint. They keep their paints in two containers made of animal skins. The paints are made from a mixture of crushed red ochre, coal, and animal fat. Right now they are painting a life-sized bison that appears to be wounded. Three red and black arrows pierce its body. There is also a mammoth and some horses. "To be sure of having a successful hunt, we have to paint the animal we want to catch," Mabuk tells the boys.

"But why have they painted the bison and the horse and not the reindeer or deer?" asks Mabuko.

"The bison and the horse are the animals that symbolize life. The bison represents the feminine side of life and the horse represents the masculine side. Both male and female are necessary to create life. The animals' lives are as precious as our own. Without the animals, we could not live," says Mabuk.

"Young boys are brought here the first time they are going to take part in the hunt," Mabuk explains to his youngest sons. "That's how they learn what they need to know about hunting. And here they will also learn what they need to know about starting a family, as I did with your mother."

1. The central part of a narrow passageway at the end of the Altamira Cave (Spain). As in other examples of cave art, narrow passageways alternate with larger painted spaces, called "chambers."

2. In a long passageway known as the Clastres Gallery, a part of the Niaux Cave in Ariège (France), there is a series of fossilized footprints of children walking side by side, and of adults. They were left on the sand floor of the main chamber in the gallery, painted with animals about 11,000 years ago. Why did these humans go so deeply into the cave barefoot, by the light of a torch? Evidence shows that the gallery was not used for dwelling, nor for burials. Thus we could imagine that their trip into the cave had something to do with rites of initiation.

3. Detail of a large cave painting in the Black Chamber of the Niaux Cave (France).

1

2

3

4

THE MEAL

The sun is setting on the horizon. Mabuk and his sons have come out of the cave and walk toward the encampment. It is already dinnertime. When they get back to the hut, they find that their mother has lit a fire outside the entrance. She has cut up several pieces of the mammoth that Mabuk killed and is now roasting the meat over the fire.

Now Mabuk, his wife, and his sons sit down to eat. It is an important moment for everyone.

"We saw the bison cave," the boys tell their mother. "When we are older we will go back there."

"Well, for those of us here at home it was not such a good day," Mother says. "Wariak, my friend from the next hut, was not feeling well. She was moaning loudly. She must have eaten something poisonous."

Just as Mother said these words, Wariak's son walks by, looking very upset. "Mother is dead," he says.

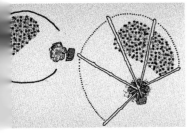

1. From the site of Mezhirich (Ukraine) 17,800 to 14,300 years ago: a roasting spit made of mammoth bones. 2. This is what a hearth might have looked like at the end of the Paleolithic age: a large hole, often round, paved and, in cases where it was more structured, lined with large stones. 3. From Dolní Vestonice (Czech Republic) about 29,000 to 25,000 years ago: a hearth with walls made of fired clay. 4. A hearth in front of a hunters' hut in Pincevent, Seine-et-Marne (France) made 15,000–11,000 years ago. The stones protect the fire from the wind.
5. Animals portrayed in cave painting of Paleolithic Europe (bison, ox, horse, ibex, reindeer, mammoth, rhinoceros, deer): these all contributed to the nutrition of Homo sapiens sapiens.

FUNERARY EQUIPMENT FOR WARIAK

"Yes, she's dead," says Mabuk when he returns from Wariak's hut. "She is not breathing. She doesn't move. Now we have to bury her. We will place her at the foot of the little hill," he says, pointing to a small hill where the sun is setting.

The boys go to dig a pit in which they will place Wariak.

The women choose the items that will be buried with Wariak: a little shell necklace, a tool made from antlers that is used for straightening arrows, some blades and arrowheads made of bone, and some red ochre powder that will be scattered in the grave and on the corpse.

"Why do we use the red powder?" asks Mabuko.

"Because it symbolizes blood, and blood means life. It will help Wariak begin her new life," Mabuk answers.

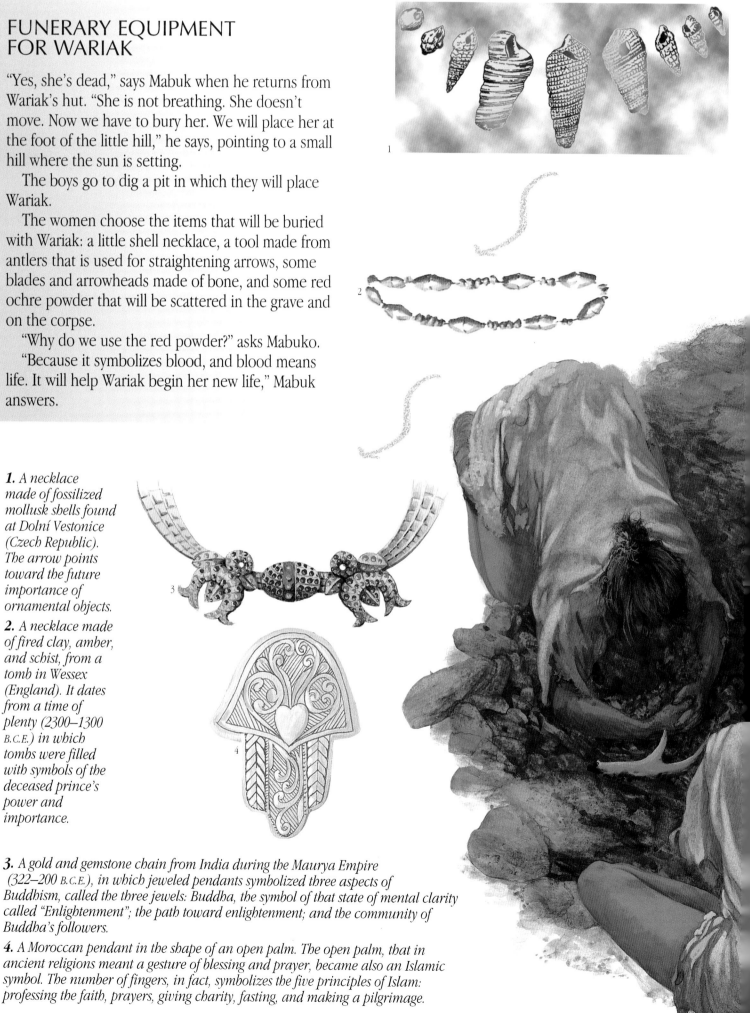

1. A necklace made of fossilized mollusk shells found at Dolní Vestonice (Czech Republic). The arrow points toward the future importance of ornamental objects.

2. A necklace made of fired clay, amber, and schist, from a tomb in Wessex (England). It dates from a time of plenty (2300–1300 B.C.E.) in which tombs were filled with symbols of the deceased prince's power and importance.

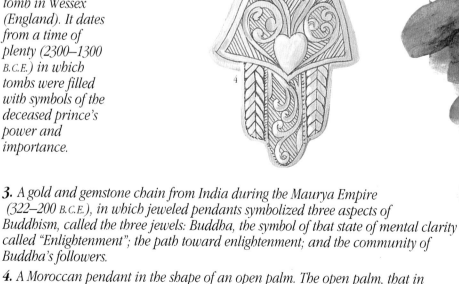

3. A gold and gemstone chain from India during the Maurya Empire (322–200 B.C.E.), in which jeweled pendants symbolized three aspects of Buddhism, called the three jewels: Buddha, the symbol of that state of mental clarity called "Enlightenment"; the path toward enlightenment; and the community of Buddha's followers.

4. A Moroccan pendant in the shape of an open palm. The open palm, that in ancient religions meant a gesture of blessing and prayer, became also an Islamic symbol. The number of fingers, in fact, symbolizes the five principles of Islam: professing the faith, prayers, giving charity, fasting, and making a pilgrimage.

5. From the Pekarna Cave in Moravia (11,000–12,400 years old): a pierced staff.

6. The drawing shows one possible use for this tool—to straighten arrows with heat.

WARIAK'S BURIAL

It is time to say good-bye to Wariak. Her husband and children have prepared a kind of stretcher, which they will use for transporting the body.

The families of the encampment walk in a sad procession and bring Wariak to her grave.

Everyone gathers around the place where she will be buried.

Then Mabuk says, "Each time a dear one leaves us, it is difficult. But we know that Wariak is starting a new life. By placing our offerings near her in the ground, we express our wish for her to go on to the next life."

After Mabuk's words, Wariak's husband and children sprinkle the red ochre in the grave and lower Wariak's body into it. They have placed the shell necklace around her neck and have placed the tools close to her. Then they sprinkle ochre on the body. Wariak's husband takes a handful of earth and tosses it onto the corpse. The others do the same. During this ceremony, one of the boys plays a sad melody on a little flute.

1

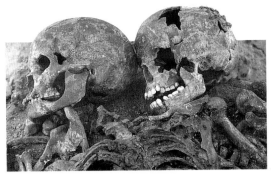

1. *Prehistoric flutes made of bone: the first one has rather crude holes for the fingers (from Isturiz, France, 30,000–27,000 years old), the second and third are more refined (from Peyrat, France, and Molodova, Ukraine, 15,000–11,000 years old).*

2. *In Italy, along the coast near the French border, 18 caves were found, the Grimaldi Caves, rich in prehistoric finds, especially burials. Here is a reconstruction of one of the graves.*

3. *The Cave of the Children, one of the Grimaldi Caves, has four graves dating from about 18,000 years ago. Here we see the skulls found in a double grave. The arrow points to later examples of rituals connected with death.*

4. *A spectacular scene of the solemn ceremony of transporting the deceased, from the end of the Paleolithic age, found at Zisah Gorge in the Brandenberg Mountains (Namibia).*

5. *In the middle of a large engraved rock in Val Camonica (Italy), a funerary scene from the fourth millennium B.C.E.: a row of human figures approach the lying corpse, which is surrounded by objects that will probably be placed in the grave.*

6. *A canoe, painted in a cave in Santa Barbara, California. The Chumash Indians, who populated this part of California between 9,000 and 500 years ago, were strongly tied to the sea. Their canoes were technological marvels. The sea and boats were symbols of the deceased person's last journey.*

ASKING THE HEAVENS

The sun has set. The first stars are shining in the sky, but not all the stars are visible because the full moon lights up the evening shadows.

Mabuk and his family are sitting in their hut, by the dim light of a lamp.

"We have had a good day," says Mabuko, the oldest son. "We have seen so many new things."

Mabuk's wife adds, "Today Wariak died . . ."

And Mabuk says, "Who knows, maybe by now Wariak is traveling through the heavens . . ."

"Father," interrupts Mabuko, "do you think that every star in the sky could be someone who has lived on the earth?"

"Perhaps," Mabuk replies. "At night, the stars keep us company."

"And so does the moon," adds Mabuko.

"Yes," says Mabuk, "the moon is never the same size. It is small, then it gets bigger, then it becomes small again, and then it disappears. Maybe it is just doing that to keep our attention."

"And the sun?" asks the youngest boy.

Mabuk answers, "The sun is the great source of light that never changes. It only changes its place on the horizon. Without its light and heat we would not be able to see, hunt, or live. The one who is in the heavens moves the shining stars, and the stars give us light and keep us company."

1. *Part of a tooth from a mammoth found in Gonzi (Ukraine) from about 14,600 years ago. The engraving has been interpreted as representing the four phases of the moon. The arrow points to later scenes related to the observation of stars.*

2. *From the rock art of Chaco Canyon (New Mexico): an engraving that represents the explosion (in 1054) of a supernova, a star that suddenly becomes extremely bright and then dies.*

3. *From the Mayan codex called the Dresda (twelfth century): the representation of a solar eclipse. The star, shown on a half-black, half-white background and hanging under a bar-shaped sky, is about to be devoured by a dragon with open jaws.*

4. *A modern radio telescope catches intense radio waves that are emitted from the Granchio Nebula, which came out of the remains of the supernova of 1054.*

GLOSSARY

Using a hollow tube a Paleolithic artist climbing a makeshift ladder, is ready to blow some color powder on the cave walls.

Two hunters, armed with spears and hidden behind boulders and shrubs, aim for a large-horned deer.

BLADE: A long, narrow, and thin flake of stone with parallel sides, usually struck from a prepared core; it has a sharp working edge. We usually call BLADE the tool *more* than 5 centimeters long, and BLADELET or MICROBLADE the tool *less* than 5 centimeters long.

BURIN: A flake or blade stone tool with a small, angled chisel edge or a sharp, beaked point.

CULTURE: In the field of prehistory, the ability to modify nature intentionally, to control or transform the environment, to acquire and transmit knowledge, to know how to benefit from experience, and to express one's own internal world beyond the needs of everyday life.

DNA: A substance (deoxyribonucleic acid) found in cells that is responsible for the transmission of hereditary characteristics.

EVOLUTION: The gradual transformation of species of animals or plants. Some scientists also accept episodes of faster and/or discontinuous evolution.

FLAKE: Roughly short and wide tool obtained from a nucleus of stone by percussion.

FLINT: Sedimentary rock formed by the accumulation of various types of deposits. It was very useful in prehistoric tool making because of its fine grain and hardness.

FOSSIL: From the Latin word meaning "to dig." One actually needs to dig to find fossils, which are evidence of ancient living organisms preserved in layers of rock. Traces of prehistoric human activity, such as deposits of stones or bones, artifacts, imprints and footprints, all belong to the world of fossils.

FOSSILIZATION: A natural process of preservation made possible by the coming together of various favorable circumstances and phenomena linked to the nature of the organism and environmental conditions.

FUNERARY EQUIPMENT: Ensembles of objects placed in graves that expressed man's feelings about death and his desire to transcend it.

GLACIATION: Cold geological period characterized by vast extensions of ice in regions of the Northern Hemisphere.

HAMMER: Stone tool, chosen for its shape and resistance, used to strike sharply a nucleus in order to detach a flake from it. (See also

HARPOON: A weapon with a pointed end and one or more series of barbs designed to catch prey. It was fixed to a shaft and used for fishing.

HOMINID: A fossil form that relates, directly or indirectly, to human evolution, be it before the dawn of human life (*Australopithecus*) or after (*Homo habilis, Homo erectus, Homo sapiens*).

HOMO ERECTUS: The type of human who lived between 1.6 million and 150,000 years ago.

Men marching along a passageway near an ice cap. They protected themselves from the cold by wearing heavy animal pelts.

HOMO HABILIS: A species of *Homo* who lived from 2.5 to 2 million years ago, to 1.6 million years ago, characterized by development of the brain, stone industry, and dwelling technology.

HOMO SAPIENS: A human more evolved than *Homo erectus*. There were three forms of *Homo Sapiens* linked with evidence that has been found dating from 100,000 to 10,000 years ago: the very ancient and extinct *Homo sapiens antiquus;* a more specialized but also extinct *Homo sapiens neanderthalensis;* and finally, one who is not different from humans as we know them today, *Homo sapiens sapiens*.

HORN: The material that makes up the horns of the oxen, deer, goat, and sheep families. It was used by *Homo sapiens sapiens* to make useful and decorative objects.

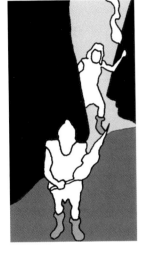

Early humans entered caves with awe and caution. The light of the torch banished the darkness inside.

INDUSTRY (PREHISTORIC): Items that early humans made from flint, bone, and horn that had an intentional use.

INITIATION: A rite in which the young people in the group are educated about the mysteries of life and nature. It has been theorized that the wall paintings in caves of the Upper Paleolithic period might have something to do with initiation.

IVORY: The material that makes up mammoth or elephant tusks used for engraving and sculpture.

LAYER: In zoology, each manifestation of the male deer's antlers.

NEANDERTHAL: See HOMO SAPIENS.

NEOLITHIC: Later Stone Age, which falls between the tenth and fourth millennia B.C.E. This age witnessed the beginning of agriculture, breeding, the production of ceramics, and the first permanent villages.

NUCLEUS (or CORE): Block of stone from which many kinds of tools are made.

PALEOLITHIC: Early Stone Age (700,000 to 10,000 years ago). Scientists divide it into three parts. The Lower Paleolithic took place 700,000 to 120,000 years ago. The presence of *Homo erectus* covers this entire time span, but it actually begins much earlier, 1.6 million years ago, in the Archeolithic era, which is characterized by Oldowan industry (choppers and chopping tools). The Middle Paleolithic took place 120,000 to 40,000 years ago, and the Upper Paleolithic took place 40,000 to 10,000 years ago.

In the lamplight, an early artist paints with various colored substances he has prepared in advance.

PERCUSSION: A strong blow with which a nucleus of stone is being hit to break off a flake. This can be done *directly* with a stone or horn hammer, or *indirectly* by putting another stone between the nucleus and the hammer, or even with *pressure* from a tool called a retoucher.

Two hunters get ready to test the quality of the tip of a spear.

PIERCED STAFF (or COMMANDING STAFF): A tool made of deer horn with one or more holes, probably used to straighten arrows that were first heated over fire, or as a buckle for garments. It can also be a symbol of authority.

PLEISTOCENE: A period of the Quaternary era characterized by glaciations. It began 1.8 million years ago and continued until 10,000 years ago. It was followed by a post-glacial period, the Holocene, which comprises the last 10,000 years.

POINT: A small stone tool with a sharp end worked from splinters or blades.

PROPITIATORY MAGIC (RITE): A ceremony intended to bring about a good result—example, successful hunting. Through magic, a technique practiced by specialists, men hoped to gain the favor of a non-physical being thought to control certain forces of nature.

SPEAR THROWER (or ATLATL): A tool made of bone or wood that is used to hurl a spear a long distance. It is made up of a hilt with a flattened end and a hook, so that when it is launched the projectile detaches from the base.

RED OCHRE: A substance dug out of accumulations of earth containing a variety of hematite, an iron mineral, that can be used as a pigment.

REMAINS: From the Latin word meaning "found," these are objects discovered during systematic archaeological investigations.

Deer hunting with a bow and arrow was an innovation in weapons technology.

RITE: An individual or group repeated act charged with symbolic references, sometimes to realities beyond this world.

SHAMAN: An individual who is capable of making contact with the supernatural world in order to help the community confront the hardships of daily life.

SITE: Place where remains of prehistoric human and their activities have been found. Such remains, discovered by scientists during a series of archaeological excavations, are then passed on to the next stage of research.

SYMBOL: A mark, sound, or object that has value and meaning beyond its material aspect. The visible reality has reference to something that is part of humans' imaginary world.

TORUS: Strong protrusion of bone. The "supraorbital torus," or visor, refers to the browridge. The "occipital torus" refers to the occipital bone in the back of the skull.

A hunter holds the new, powerful weapon that will make it easier for him to hunt big game: the spear thrower.

INDEX

Page numbers in *italics* refer to illustrations.

Altamira cave, Spain, 12, 17, *33*, 33, *34*
Animals, 13, 14, 20–23, *21*, *23*, 29, 34
Antlers, 22, 31
Apache Indians, 26
Apollo 11, South Namibia, 13
Australia, 16, 17

Beringia, 14, 15
Bering Strait, 15, 16
Black Sea, 9
Brain, evolution of, 16, *16*
Brandenberg Mountains, Namibia, 41
Brassempouy, Lande, France, 30
Buddhism, 38

Cave of the Children, 41
Cave paintings, 11–13, *12*, *13*, *17*, 17, *34*, 34, *35*, 37, *37*
Chaco Canyon, New Mexico, 42
Chiucchiari, Potenza, Italy, 33
Chumash Indians, 41
Continuity theory, 10
Cordilleran glaciers, 14, 15
Cro-Magnon "Old Man," *8*, 9

Dance, 26, *26*
DNA analysis, 10
Dong Son, Vietnam, 33
Dordogne, France, 9, 30
Dresda, 42

El Cingle de la Mola Remigia, Spain, 12
Endocranial casts, 16
Eskimo, 14

Fertility cults, 30
Fire, use of, 13
Fishing, 25
Flint, 11
Flutes, 40, *41*, 41
Food, 13, 26, 29, 37
Funeral practices, 12, 38, *38*, 40, *41*, 41

Glaciers, 14, 15
Grimaldi caves, Italy, 41

Har kakom plateau, Sinai peninsula, 26
Harpoons, *10*, 10, 11, 20, *20*, *24*, 24, 25
Homo erectus, 8
   brain of, 16, *16*
Homo habilis
   brain of, 16, *16*
Homo sapiens antiquus, 9
Homo sapiens sapiens
   brain of, 16, *16*
   cave paintings of, 11–13, *12*, *13*, *17*, 17, 34, *34*, *35*, *37*, 37
   caves of, 11, *32*, *33*, 33, *34*, 34
   evolution of, 10
   food and, 13, 26, 29, 37
   funeral practices of, 12, *38*, 38, 40, 41, *41*
   hunting and gathering lifestyle of, 13
   hunting by, 20, 22, 25
   huts of, *22*, 22, 26, *26*, 27
   migration of, 9, 15
   skull of, *9*, 9, *16*, 16
   tools and weapons of, *10*, 10–11, 20, *20*, 24, *24*, 25, *29*, 29–31, *30*, 39, *39*
Huts, *22*, 22, 26, *26*, 27

Ice Age, 14–16
Indonesia, 17
Islam, 38

Java, 16, 17
Javelins, *11*, 11, *20*, 20

Kostienki, Russia, 11
Kow Swamp, Australia, 16

Lamps and torches, *32*, 33
Laurentide glaciers, 14, 15
Laussel, Dordogne, France, 30
Lepenski Vir, Yugoslavia, 24
Licinia, 24

Mal'ta Irkutsk, Siberia, 22
Mammoths, 20–23, *21*, *23*, 29

Manzanares River, Spain, 21
Maternity cults, 30
Maurya Empire, 38
Meiendorf, Germany, 24
Mezhirich, Ukraine, 22, 37
Milovice, Southern Moravia, 23
Molodova, Ukraine, 41

Na-Dene Indians, 14
Neanderthals, 9, 10, 12
Niaux cave, Ariège, France, 28, 34, *35*

Oblazowa cave, Poland, 28

Paints, 34
Paleo-Indians, 14
Paleolithic rock art, 12, *12*
Pekarna cave, Moravia, 24, 39
Peyrat, France, 41
Pincevent, Seine-et-Marne, France, 37
Pleistocene period, 16
Proto-Aleutians, 14

Qafzeh, Israel, 9

Racó de Molero, Spain, 12

Senufo tribe, 24
"Sistine Chapel of Prehistory, The," 17
Skhul, Israel, 9
"Sorcerer, The," 12, *12*
Stars, 42, *43*
Substitution theory, 10

Tepexpán, Mexico, 16
Timonovka, Russia, 23
Tools, *10*, 10–11, *29*, 29, *30*, 30, 31, *39*, 39
Turkey, 9

Val Camonica, Italy, 26, 41
Venus with the Hood, *30*, 30

Weapons, *10*, 10, *11*, 11, *20*, 20, *24*, 24, 25
Wessex, England, 38

Yukon territory, 14, 15

Zisah Gorge, Namibia, 41

PICTURE CREDITS

*The number in boldface refers to the page and
the number in parentheses refers to the illustration.*

EMMANUEL ANATI: **26** (1). Jean Clottes: **35** (3) EDITORIALE JACA BOOK (Giorgio Bacchin): **38** (4); (Daniela Balloni): **11** (5), **14–15**, **17** (7, 8); (Remo Berselli): **16** (2); (Sandro Corsi): **43** (4); (Giacinto Gaudenzi): **32** (3), **38** (3); (Maria Elena Gonano): **11** (7, 8); (Umberto L. Levi); **20** (1); (Antonio Molino): **10** (2, 3, 4), **30** (1), **38** (2); (Carlo Scotti): **9** (3); (Angelo Stabin): **41** (2, 3). RODNEY HOOK: **10** (1). MUSÉE DE L'HOMME (J. Oster): **8** (1). PEDRO A. SAURA RAMOS: **17** (6), **33** (5), **34** (1).

Illustration sources faithfully reproduced or modified

Anati, Emmanuel. *The Camunians. To the Roots of European Civilization.* Jaca Book, 1979: **41** (5).

——. *The Imaginary Museum of Prehistory. Rock Art of the World.* Jaca Book, 2002: **27** (5, 6, 7).

——.*Origins of Art and Conceptuality.* Jaca Book, 1989: **12** (1, 3, 4), **41** (4).

Beltrán, Antonio, edited by. *The Prehistoric Altamira Cave.* Photo by Pedro A. Saura Ramos. Jaca Book, Milano/Lunwerg, Madrid, 1998: **12** (2).

Clottes, Jean, and Robert Simmonet. "Recent Studies in a Deep Cave. The René Clastre Gallery in the Pyrenees," in *The Human Adventure,* Jaca Book, Year 5, No. 16, Winter, 1990–Spring, 1991: **28** (1), **35** (2).

Crippa, Maria Antonietta, and Mahmoud Zibawi. *Paleo Christian Art.* Jaca Book, 1998: **32** (4).

Dué, Andrea, edited by. *The First Inhabited Lands. From Primates to Homo Sapiens,* vol. 1 of *The Atlases of the History of Mankind.* Jaca Book, 1993: **30** (2, 4), **32** (1), **39** (6).

——, edited by. *In Prehistoric Times,* Vol. 1 of *The Historical Atlases. Man and the Environment.* Jaca Book, 1997: **36** (1).

Facchini, Fiorenzo. *The Path of Human Evolution.* Jaca Book, 1994: **8** (2), **16** (1).

——.*Origins: Man. Introduction to Paleoanthropology.* Jaca Book, 1990: **16** (3, 4, 5), **26** (2), **27** (3), **29** (3), **30** (3).

——, edited by. *Paleoanthropology and Prehistory,* a volume of *The Open Thematic Encyclopedia.* Jaca Book, 1993: **20** (2), **22** (1), **37** (5).

Facchini, Fiorenzo, M. Gimbutas, J. K. Kozlowski, and B.Van-Dermeersch. *Religiosity in Prehistoric Times.* Jaca Book, 1991: **24** (5).

Kozlowski, Janusz K. *The Prehistory of Eastern European Art.* Jaca Book, 1992: **11** (6), **23** (3), **24** (1, 2, 3, 4), **29** (2), **38** (1), **39** (5).

——."The Mammoth Hunters" in *The Human Adventure.* Jaca Book, Year 5, No. 17, Summer, 1991: **23** (4).

Lee, Georgia. *A Day with a Chumash Indian.* Jaca Book, 1998: **41** (6).

Lewis-Williams, James David. *The Art of the Savanna. Southern African Rock Paintings.* Jaca Book, 1983: **13** (5).

Maioli, Walter. *Origins: Sound and Music.* Jaca Book, 1991: **40** (1).

Schobinger, Juan. *The Art of the First Americans.* Jaca Book, 1997: **27** (4).

*Other pictures not mentioned here come from the Jaca Book archives.
Giorgio Bacchin is the author of those tables not mentioned here.*